A summary of the life of St. Werburgh. With an historical account of the images upon her shrine, (now the episcopal throne) in the choir of Chester. Collected from ancient chronicles, and old writers. By a citizen of Chester. ...

William Cowper

PRINT EDITIONS

A summary of the life of St. Werburgh. With an historical account of the images upon her shrine, (now the episcopal throne) in the choir of Chester. Collected from ancient chronicles, and old writers. By a citizen of Chester. ...

Cowper, William
ESTCID: T065474
Reproduction from British Library
A Citizen of Chester = William Cowper.
Chester : printed by Eliz. Adams; and sold by the booksellers in that city, 1749.
31,[1]p. ; 4°

Eighteenth Century
Collections Online
Print Editions

Gale ECCO Print Editions

Relive history with *Eighteenth Century Collections Online*, now available in print for the independent historian and collector. This series includes the most significant English-language and foreign-language works printed in Great Britain during the eighteenth century, and is organized in seven different subject areas including literature and language; medicine, science, and technology; and religion and philosophy. The collection also includes thousands of important works from the Americas.

The eighteenth century has been called "The Age of Enlightenment." It was a period of rapid advance in print culture and publishing, in world exploration, and in the rapid growth of science and technology – all of which had a profound impact on the political and cultural landscape. At the end of the century the American Revolution, French Revolution and Industrial Revolution, perhaps three of the most significant events in modern history, set in motion developments that eventually dominated world political, economic, and social life.

In a groundbreaking effort, Gale initiated a revolution of its own: digitization of epic proportions to preserve these invaluable works in the largest online archive of its kind. Contributions from major world libraries constitute over 175,000 original printed works. Scanned images of the actual pages, rather than transcriptions, recreate the works *as they first appeared.*

Now for the first time, these high-quality digital scans of original works are available via print-on-demand, making them readily accessible to libraries, students, independent scholars, and readers of all ages.

For our initial release we have created seven robust collections to form one the world's most comprehensive catalogs of 18th century works.

Initial Gale ECCO Print Editions collections include:

History and Geography
Rich in titles on English life and social history, this collection spans the world as it was known to eighteenth-century historians and explorers. Titles include a wealth of travel accounts and diaries, histories of nations from throughout the world, and maps and charts of a world that was still being discovered. Students of the War of American Independence will find fascinating accounts from the British side of conflict.

Social Science

Delve into what it was like to live during the eighteenth century by reading the first-hand accounts of everyday people, including city dwellers and farmers, businessmen and bankers, artisans and merchants, artists and their patrons, politicians and their constituents. Original texts make the American, French, and Industrial revolutions vividly contemporary.

Medicine, Science and Technology

Medical theory and practice of the 1700s developed rapidly, as is evidenced by the extensive collection, which includes descriptions of diseases, their conditions, and treatments. Books on science and technology, agriculture, military technology, natural philosophy, even cookbooks, are all contained here.

Literature and Language

Western literary study flows out of eighteenth-century works by Alexander Pope, Daniel Defoe, Henry Fielding, Frances Burney, Denis Diderot, Johann Gottfried Herder, Johann Wolfgang von Goethe, and others. Experience the birth of the modern novel, or compare the development of language using dictionaries and grammar discourses.

Religion and Philosophy

The Age of Enlightenment profoundly enriched religious and philosophical understanding and continues to influence present-day thinking. Works collected here include masterpieces by David Hume, Immanuel Kant, and Jean-Jacques Rousseau, as well as religious sermons and moral debates on the issues of the day, such as the slave trade. The Age of Reason saw conflict between Protestantism and Catholicism transformed into one between faith and logic -- a debate that continues in the twenty-first century.

Law and Reference

This collection reveals the history of English common law and Empire law in a vastly changing world of British expansion. Dominating the legal field is the *Commentaries of the Law of England* by Sir William Blackstone, which first appeared in 1765. Reference works such as almanacs and catalogues continue to educate us by revealing the day-to-day workings of society.

Fine Arts

The eighteenth-century fascination with Greek and Roman antiquity followed the systematic excavation of the ruins at Pompeii and Herculaneum in southern Italy; and after 1750 a neoclassical style dominated all artistic fields. The titles here trace developments in mostly English-language works on painting, sculpture, architecture, music, theater, and other disciplines. Instructional works on musical instruments, catalogs of art objects, comic operas, and more are also included.

The BiblioLife Network

This project was made possible in part by the BiblioLife Network (BLN), a project aimed at addressing some of the huge challenges facing book preservationists around the world. The BLN includes libraries, library networks, archives, subject matter experts, online communities and library service providers. We believe every book ever published should be available as a high-quality print reproduction; printed on-demand anywhere in the world. This insures the ongoing accessibility of the content and helps generate sustainable revenue for the libraries and organizations that work to preserve these important materials.

The following book is in the "public domain" and represents an authentic reproduction of the text as printed by the original publisher. While we have attempted to accurately maintain the integrity of the original work, there are sometimes problems with the original work or the micro-film from which the books were digitized. This can result in minor errors in reproduction. Possible imperfections include missing and blurred pages, poor pictures, markings and other reproduction issues beyond our control. Because this work is culturally important, we have made it available as part of our commitment to protecting, preserving, and promoting the world's literature.

GUIDE TO FOLD-OUTS MAPS and OVERSIZED IMAGES

The book you are reading was digitized from microfilm captured over the past thirty to forty years. Years after the creation of the original microfilm, the book was converted to digital files and made available in an online database.

In an online database, page images do not need to conform to the size restrictions found in a printed book. When converting these images back into a printed bound book, the page sizes are standardized in ways that maintain the detail of the original. For large images, such as fold-out maps, the original page image is split into two or more pages

Guidelines used to determine how to split the page image follows:

• Some images are split vertically; large images require vertical and horizontal splits.
• For horizontal splits, the content is split left to right.
• For vertical splits, the content is split from top to bottom.
• For both vertical and horizontal splits, the image is processed from top left to bottom right.

The GENEALOGY of the KINGS of *MERCIA*

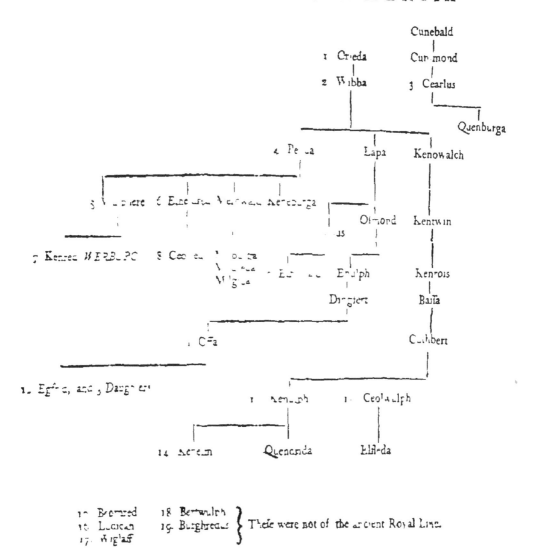

A
SUMMARY
OF THE
Life of St. *Werburgh*.

With an Hiftorical Account

OF THE

Images upon Her SHRINE,

(Now the Epifcopal Throne)

In the CHOIR of *CHESTER*.

Collected from ancient Chronicles, and old Writers.

By a Citizen of CHESTER.

The *Manufcript* being given to the BLUE-COAT-SCHOOL, is publifhed
by the TREASURERS for the Benefit of that CHARITY.

—————————————————*Figuras*

Retulit antiquas—————————

OVID. Met.

CHESTER:

Printed by ELIZ. ADAMS ; and Sold by the Bookfellers in
that City. 1749.

INTRODUCTION.

CUSTOM having now made it almoſt neceſſary, that a Sort of Preface or Introduction, ſhould precede even the ſlighteſt Performance, a few Lines ſhall therefore premiſe ſomewhat concerning the following Pages.

The Chapter of *Cheſter* having lately begun to beautify their Cathedral, the decayed Decorations on the Epiſcopal Throne engaged their Attention. This fine Piece of Antiquity had been ornamented with Carving and Statuary, both which had greatly ſuffered, not by Time, but by Violence. They have therefore endeavoured to repair the one, and to reſtore the other, ſo that the little IMAGES which have for ſo many Centuries guarded, as it were, this ancient Monument, and were ſo injuriouſly defaced, are, by a commendable Care, now made whole again.

As the Perfonages whom Thefe fhould reprefent, lived in the early Ages of Chriftianity, they are but little known to us, which induced One, who refpects Antiquities, to extract from old Writers fome Account of them, this was done in a very few Days, for his own Amufement. He has fince been prevailed upon to let his Collections be publifhed for the Information of others, as likewife to contribute a Mite to a very laudable Charity. And as they go to the Prefs, with thefe Intentions only, they may therefore hope for a candid Reception.

CHESTER,
7*'s 1 174*.

The Names of some AUTHORS cited in these COLLECTIONS.

Anglia Sacra

Bede
Bradshaw
Brompton

Camden

Dugdale

Florence *of* Worcester

Goscelin

Higden

Henry *of* Huntingdon.

Ingulphus

Langhorn's *Chronicle*

Sir Peter Leycester
Leland's *Collection*

Malmsbury

Powell's *History of* Wales

Saxon Chronicle
Simeon *of* Durham
Speed
Spelman's *Councils*

Tyrrell.

A SUMMARY of the
Life of St. WERBURGH, &c.

THE Episcopal Throne, in the Cathedral-Church of *Chester*, allowed to be the Shrine of St. *Werburgha*, to whom the Abbey was dedicated, is a Stone Structure in the antique monumental Stile, of an oblong quadrangular Form, eight Feet and nine Inches in Height, in Length from East to West seven Feet and six Inches, in Breadth from North to South four Feet and eight Inches, ornamented with six Gothic Arches (three Feet and four Inches in Height) two towards the North Front, two towards the South, one at the East End, and the other at the West, above each of these is an Arch, representing a Window, in the same Stile of Architecture.

This Fabrick is decorated with Variety of Carving, and embellished with a Number of Images, about fourteen Inches in

C   Height,

Height, in different Habits, beautified with Painting and Gild-
ing Each of these held in one Hand a Scroll or Label, upon
which were inscribed in *Latin*, but in the Old *English* Character, the Names of Kings and Saints of the Royal Line of
MERCIA Many of the Labels are broke off, others are so
much defaced, that only a Syllable or two can be read.

These Statues are placed in the following Order, if we begin
with the Figure at the South-west Angle, fronting the West,
and thence proceed over that End, along the North Front, and
thence round the East End, towards the Stairs up to the
Throne.

1	Rex CRIEDA.	16	Rex - - - - - - DUS
2	Rex PENDA	17	Sta - - - - - - - - RGA
3	Rex WOLPHERUS	18	- - - - - - - - - US.
4	Rex CEOLREDUS.	19.	- - - - - - - - -
5	- - - - - - - - -	20	BALDREDUS.
6.	Rex OFFA.	21	MERWALDUS.
7	Rex EGFERTUS	22.	Rex WIGLAFF.
8	- - - - - - - - -	23.	Rex BERTWULPH.
9	St KENELMUS	24	Rex BURGHREDUS.
10	St MILBURGA.	25	- - - - - - - - -
11	Rex BEORNA	26.	Sa - - - - - - - EDA
12	Rex COLWLPHUS	27	- - - - - - - -
13	- - - - - - - - -	28	- - - - - - - -
14	St - - - - - - LDA.	29	Rex ETHELBERTUS
15	- - - - - - - - S	30.	Sta MILDRIDA.

Four more Images have been quite cut away, two at the West,
and two at the East End.

The

The Perfonages which were intended to be reprefented by thefe Statues, were either her Anceftors, or elfe moft of them nearly related to St. *Werburgha*, who was Daughter of *Wulphere*, King of *Mercia*, by his Queen *Erminilda*. She was (1) in her Infancy (according to the Cuftom of thofe Times) be- Langhorn's Chronicle trothed, or married to her Coufin-German *Ceolredus*, afterwards King of *Mercia*; (2) yet notwithftanding her Marriage, fhe kept herfelf a Virgin, chafte and inviolate, having been bred by her Mother *Erminilda*, in the Fear of God, and a Contempt of all worldly Vanities, fhe very early formed a Refolution to dedi- Gofcelinus in vita Sanctæ Werburghæ, cate herfelf to God in a State of Religion and Virginity.

She perfifted in this Intention, not only during the Time of Marriage, but after her Husband's Deceafe, (3) notwithftanding many great Matches were propofed to her Nor could fhe be prevailed upon by her Father to alter her Refolution, tho', whilft he lived, he would not fuffer her to be profeffed. (4) But

---

(1) " Quæ adhuc puellula, nupta Ceolredo, " more temporum, virginitatem confervavit " illibatam, et poft obitum mariti velata eft, " cum matre Erminilda apud Hely, fub " Sancta Etheldreda abbatiffa, Erminildæ " matertera ' *Langhorn Chron*

(2) Notwithftanding that the concurrent Teftimonies of feveral Authors declare her to have been the Wife of *Ceolredus*, yet the Diftance of fixty fix Years between the Times of their Deceafe, may poffibly occafion fomewhat of a Doubt But any thing of that Kind will be eafily folved, if we confider that fhe was a very young Girl (*Puellula*) when fhe was married to this Prince, who lived to be, at leaft, a middle-aged Man, as he did not immediately fucceed his Father in the Throne of *Mercia*, but had the Kingdom after his Coufin *Kenred*, and enjoved it eight Years He died A D 716,

and fhe died A D 782 *Sax Chron*

(3) Werbodus vir magni nominis apud Wulfherum regem, Merciorum ambiebat Werburgam in uxorem *Bradfhaw, in vita Sanctæ Werburghæ*, L 1

(4) " Werburgha poft mortem Wulpheri " patris fui intravit monafterium de Ely, " cujus fanctitatem cum Etheldredus rex " Merciorum, ejus patruus cognoviffet, ab " ductam ex Ely principatum monafteriorum ' fanctimonialium, quæ in ejus regno erant, " ei tradidit " *Lelandi Collectanea*

(4) " Werburgham fanctimonialem præ- " fecit patruus rex Etheldredus quibufdam " virginum monafteriis,—fcil apud Trick- " ingham, Wednam, et Hamburgam, fed " apud primam obiit, apud tertiam, ut ipfa " vivens jufferat, fepulta eft, ubi ufque ad- " ventum Danorum incorrupta jacuit *Higden*

after

after the Death of *Wulphere*, she and her Mother *Ermenilda*
were veiled by S⁺ *Etheldreda*, Abbess of *Ely* (1) Her
Uncle, King *Etheldred*, who succeeded his Brother *Wulphere*,
admiring his Neice's eminent Piety, and being much dissatisfied
that his Kingdom should be deprived of such a Pattern of Religion and Virtue, made the most pressing Applications to her,
to quit *Ely*, and return to her native Country She was at
length prevailed upon to come back into *Mercia*, and to accept
the Superintendency of several religious Virgin-Societies, *viz.*
the Monasteries of *Trickingham* (now *Trentham*) in *Staffordshire*, *Weedon*, in *Northamptonshire*, and *Hanbury*, in *Staffordshire* At the first of these Places she died, and (according
to her Desire, when living) was buried at the last, where her
Body remained entire and incorrupt for almost one hundred
Years.

Malmesbury (*de gestis regum*, L. 1 Ch. 4) says, that she
died and was buried at *Chester*, but *Higden* tells us, that her
Remains were deposited at *Hanbury* (near *Tutbury*) in *Staffordshire*, and (2) that in the Year 875, when the *Danes* had
ravaged a great Part of *Mercia*, and were advanced as far as
(3) *Repton* in *Derbyshire*, the People of *Hanbury*, terrified
with their Devastations, took up the Corps of St. *Werburgh*,

---

Decrevit Werburga virgo, u
... ... monasterio
... ... Ecclesiae
... Deum venerari ... Reperdoniam
... Hamburgensi ... reg
... ... Reperdon
... ... corpus San
Werburga ... accednnm

... per usque nunc incorruptum, cum se-
... comes beatæ virginis continente, ad
Legeceastram (quæ nunc Cestria dicitur)
unquam ad locum tutissimum contra stra-
gem barbaricam transierunt *Ibid ad*
Ann. 8

Erroneously call'd *Ripten* by Mr
Cave Vol I p 21.

which

which they found frefh and entire, and carried it in a Hearfe to *Chefter*, as a Place of Safety, from the Havock and Barbarities of the *Danes*.

We do not find from any of the old Writers, about what Time her Shrine was erected, but fhall endeavour to give fome Account of Thofe, whofe Statues are carved upon it.

CRIEDA. This Prince was derived, by (1) about ten Defcents from *Woden*, the famous Stem and Origin of the *Saxons*, and indeed the common Father of the northern Nations. He came into *Britain*, A. D 584, and founded the Sovereignty of *Mercia*, which by the Conquefts, and Acquifitions of his Succeffors, became afterwards the moft powerful Kingdom of the *Saxon Heptarchy*, having for its Boundaries, *Humber* on the North, the *Severn* on the Weft, the *Thames* on the South, and on the Eaft the Kingdoms of *Effex* and of the *Eaft-Angles*. It confifted of *Chefhire*, *Derbyfhire*, *Nottinghamfhire*, *Staffordfhire*, *Shropfhire*, *Northamptonfhire*, *Leicefterfhire*, *Lincolnfhire*, *Huntingdonfhire*, *Rutlandfhire*, *Warwickfhire*, *Worcefterfhire*, *Oxfordfhire*, *Glocefterfhire*, *Buckinghamfhire*, *Bedfordfhire*, Part of *Herefordfhire*, and a fmall Portion of *Somerfetfhire*. Hiftorians have not informed us how *Crieda* firft got Poffeffion of this Kingdom, nor have they tranfmitted any thing more concerning him He died A. D 593

FIGURE I

Sax Chron

Hen of Huntingdon

Florence of Worcefter

Sax Chron

---

(1) " Crieda fuit filius Cynewoldi, Cyne-
" woldus Cnebbæ, Cnebha Iceli, Icelus
" Eomæri, Eomærus Angeltheowi, Angel

" theowus Offæ, Offa Wærmundi, Wær-
" mundus Wihtlægi, Wihtlægus Wodem —
Sax Chron, in Pindæ genealogia, ad ann 626

PENDA,

PENDA, ſurnamed *The Strong.* He was the Grandſon of *Creda*, and did not come to the Throne 'till he was Fifty Years of Age. He was of a bold, reſtleſs, and enterprizing Spirit, ever invading and ravaging the Territories of the neighbouring Princes. Having marched againſt *Oſwald*, King of the *Northumbers*, they came to a Battle at a Place called (1) *Maſerfield*, where *Oſwald* was ſlain on the fifth of *Auguſt*, A. D 642. By this Victory *Penda* made himſelf Maſter of thoſe Parts of the *Northumbrian* Dominions which lay on the South Side of the *Humber.* He then laid Siege to *Bamborough*, which had been built (2) and ſtrongly fortified by *Ida*, the firſt King of the *Northumbers.* *Penda* endeavoured to reduce it by Fire, but was baffled, and retreated.

As his whole Reign was a continued Warfare, he had, at different Times, killed in Battle five Chriſtian Kings, and though he would never be converted, yet he permitted his Son *Peada* to be baptized, and to receive Preachers and Miſſionries into his Territories. (1) *Bede* tells us, that *Penda* was wont to exprefs a great Abhorrence of thofe outfide Chriftians, who did not practife what they profeffed; declaring thofe to be contemptible Wretches, who did not ferve that God in whom they believed

Penda's chief Pleafure was in harraffing the *Northumbrians*; and having engaged in a War with King *Ofwy*, Brother, and Succeffor to *Ofwald*, they fought a bloody Battle on the fifteenth of *November*, A. D. 655, upon (2) the Banks of the River *Winnaed* (now *Aire*) near *Leeds* in *Yorkfhire*, where the *Mercians* were totally routed, and (3) *Penda*, together with thirty Chieftains of royal Extraction, killed upon the Spot. He was flain in the eightieth Year of his Age, having reigned thirty Years.

Bede, l iii c 24

WULPHERE, the fecond Son of *Penda*. He fucceeded his elder Brother *Peada*, who was poifoned by his Wife, a *Northumbrian* Princefs, in the third Year of his Reign.

FIG 3
Leland Coll vol I p 211

Wulphere, during his Infancy, had been concealed, preferved, and afterwards fet upon the Throne of *Mercia*, by the Care and Affection of three Nobleman Soon after his Acceffion, he renounced Paganifm, was baptized, and caufed his Children to be educated in the Chriftian Religion

<hr />

1 Penda rex odio habebat et defti nd. con. eio h.e Chri time o opu re ndo non il ar d profeff e con eorn ndo effe os et m feros qui Deo tuo r e iem cre er e d e con n ere i i

2 The Place was afterwards called Win winfield or the Field of Win,

3 Hoc no Penda peia in Winw feld, et e prole Regia cum co ex Chri d c

He was an active Prince, much embroiled with his neighbouring Potentates, and waged War with various Success. He was attacked by *Kenwalch*, King of the *West-Saxons*, but had the good Fortune to defeat the Invaders, and so far improved his Victory, that he subdued *Buckinghamshire*, and the adjoining Parts of *Oxfordshire*, as far as the *Thames*, and afterwards conquered a Part of *Surry*, *Hampshire*, and the *Isle of Wight*. Having fought and vanquished *Adelwalch*, King of the *South-Saxons*, he brought him Prisoner into *Mercia*, where he was converted to Christianity, upon which *Wulphere* restored him to his Liberty, (1) and gave him the *Isle of Wight*, and a large District in *Hampshire*.

Malmesbury charges *Wulphere* with simonically selling the Bishoprick of *London* to one *Wina*, which, if true, serves to evince that he had got an absolute Sway in the Kingdom of *Essex*.

In the seventeenth and last Year of his Reign, he fought a bloody Battle with *Escwin* King of the *West-Saxons*, at (2) *Bedanheof*, where a terrible Slaughter was made. *Henry* of *Huntingdon* says, that if there was any Advantage gained in this Battle, it might be claimed by the *Mercian*, who died not long afterwards.

Wulphere married *Erminilda*, Princess of *Kent* (3) Their chief Residence was near *Stone* in *Staffordshire*, and by her he had Issue a Daughter, *Werburgh*, and three Sons, two of

which

which died before him, (some Writers say, killed by him) but the third, *Kenred*, came afterwards to be King of *Mercia.*

CEOLRED, Nephew of *Wulphere*, Cousin-German, and (according to the (1) *Saxon* Chronicle) Husband to (1) St. *Werburgha*, whose Brother *Kenred* resigned to him the Kingdom of *Mercia.* FIG 4.

In the Year 7ɪ5, he fought a memorable Battle with *Ina*, King of the *West-Saxons*, at *Wodensburgh* in *Wiltshire*, but the Occasions of this War are not related by any Historian. *Henry* of *Huntingdon* tells us, that it was a bloody Engagement, and so fatal to both Sides, that it was hard to say which had suffered most. Little else is recorded of this Prince. He was reputed to be of an active, warlike Disposition, and had a great Character He died in the ninth Year of his Reign, A. D. 716, and was interred at *Litchfield.* Sax Chron

Ibid

OFFA. A Prince of the ancient Lineage of *Woden*, and of the Royal House of *Mercia*, being descended from *Eawa* (or *Eapa*) Brother of King *Penda* Grandfather to St. *Werburgha* *Offa* was called to the Throne of *Mercia* by the unanimous Voice of the People, harrassed out by the tyrannical Oppressions of the Usurper *Beorned*. He began to reign A. D. 756, and was accounted one of the greatest among the *Mercian* Monarchs. His first Exploit, after his Accession to the Throne of his Ancestors, was an Expedition against the People of *Kent*, whom FIG 6
Sax Chron
sub anno 756
Florence of
Worcester, p
274

Sax Chron

(*) Werburga, Ceolredi regina, sub anno 782.

he invaded with a powerful Force, and, after an obstinate Engagement, routed their Army, and with his own Hand, killed their King *Alric* This Battle was fought at *Otford* upon the *Darent*, A. D. ---

In the Year following, he attacked the *West-Saxons*, and defeated their King *Kinwulph*, at *Bensington* (or *Benson*) in *Oxford* ..., adjoining to *Berkshire*, and forced him to a Cession of all that Territory on the North of the *Thames* which, from that Time became a Part of the Kingdom of *Mercia* He soon afterwards subdued *Gloucestershire*, and a Part of *Somersetshire*, and founded the Abbey of *Bath* And next, to shew his great Power, attempted to remove the Archiepiscopal See from *Canterbury* and to fix it at *Lichfield*

About this Time the *Welsh* taking the Opportunity of his Wars with the *Saxons*, invaded *Mercia* with Fire and Sword, and ravaged the Country in a dreadful manner Upon which *Offa* thought it proper to come to a Truce with his other Adversaries and turning his Arms against the *Welsh*, drove them from their new Conquests, and forced them to quit to him all the plain Country between *Severn* and *Wye* which he peopled with *Saxons* and as a Boundary and Barrier against future Invasions he threw up that prodigious Trench from the Mouth of the River *D...* to that of the *Wye* extending at out ninety Miles and since called *Offa's Ditch* " This Foss is the

Right Reverend Editor of *Camden* may be seen *Brinkburn-*
" H... and near *Rhos*, or *Hay* and *Luiden* in *Hereford-*
shire, and is continued northwards from *Knighton*, over a
P... S... g ..., into *Montgomeryshire* and may be traced
" over

" over the long Mountain, called in *Welſh*, *Kevn Digolh*, to
" *Harden-Caſtle*, croſs the *Severn* and *Llan-Drinio Common*,
" from whence it paſſes *Vyrnwy* again into *Shropſhire*, not far
" from *Oſwaldſtry* where there is alſo a ſmall Village, called
" *Trevyrclawdh*. In *Denbighſhire*, it is viſible along the Road
" between *Rhyabbon* and *Wrexham*, from whence being con-
" tinued thorough *Flintſhire*, it ends a little below *Holy-well*,
" where that Water falls into the *Dee*, at a Place formerly
" the Site of *Baſingwark*" (*)

The Reputation of this Prince was raiſed to ſuch a Height,
that *Charles the Great*, (commonly called *Charlemaine*) the
moſt powerful and accompliſh'd Monarch of that Age, ſought
his Friendſhip, ſending him rich Preſents, and, upon his Account, granting conſiderable Immunities to *Engliſh* Travellers

But *Charles* had, ſoon afterwards, good Reaſon to alter his
Opinion of *Offa*'s Character, which became deeply ſtained by an
Act of moſt perfidious Cruelty. *Offa* was, by a ſolemn Treaty, Giraldus
to give his Daughter *Althrida* in Marriage to *Ethelbert*, King Cambren.
of the *Eaſt-Angles*, and accordingly that Prince came, by In-

---

(* It has been mentioned by ſome Wri-
ter, that when *Offa* had finiſh'd his Dyke,
he promulged a Decree, That if any *Welſh-
man* ſhould paſs over this Boundary, he
ſhould be puniſhed with the Loſs of his
Right Hand

This is hinted at, in a Poem publiſhed by
a young Nobleman of *Oxford*, about eight
Year ago

' *Tu potens O' m Cumb o nbrhent ferz s,*
' *—rs intc du it r d10) a 9a agg e tuffa,*

" *Et pulor abiciſſes, perrupto limite, dextra*

which may be thus tranſlated

You could great *Offa*, with deep Dykes
encloſe
Within their Bourds, your rugged *Cam-
b r* Foes
Nor dard they range into the *Mercian*
Lands,
Dreading the Doom of amputated
Hands

vitation,

...ration, into *Mercia*, where (1) *Offa*, by the Instigation of his Wife, in order to get the Kingdom of the *East-Angles*, basely broke thro' all Faith and Hospitality, and caused his royal unsuspecting Guest to be assassinated (2) by one *Grimbert*, in his Court at *Sutton-Wallis* in *Herefordshire*, upon the first Day of *May*, A D 79. The Body of (3) the murdered King was, by *Offa*'s Orders, buried at *Marden*, not far from *Hereford*, upon the Banks of the River *Lug* but was afterwards removed from thence, and deposited in *Hereford*, where the Cathedral is since built, and dedicated to his Memory

The Princes of these Times could atone for Crimes of the blackest Dye, by Pilgrimages, and Donations to Religious Uses

Offa, in order to obtain Quiet for his Conscience, set out for *Rome*, and, whilst there, granted to the *Pope*, and his Successors, that Tribute, which has been since called *Peter-pence*

Having received his Holiness' Absolution, he returned to *England*, and built and endowed the Abbey of St *Albans*, which he just lived to finish Having reigned thirty-nine Years, he died about the End of *July*, or the Beginning of *August*, A D 794

EGFERTUS (or EGFRIDUS) Son and Successor to *Offa*, a Prince of great Hopes, but soon snatched away, having reigned only one hundred and forty-one Days He was interred in the Minster of St *Albans*

St. KENELM   This Infant King was the Son of *Kenulf,* FIG 9
(1) a Prince of the *Mercian* Blood-Royal, who succeeded *Eg-
fert,* juft before mentioned.   *Kenelm* was but feven Years old
at the Death of his Father, and his own Acceffion to the Crown·
He had reigned only a few Months, when his Sifter *Quendrida*
plotted againft his Life, (2) and procured his Tutor, (one
Afcobert) to murder him, who decoying the innocent Youth
into an unfrequented Wood, cut off his Head, and buried him
under a Thorn-Tree   The Author of *Polychronicon* fays, that Higden
the Corps was thrown into a Well.   Several old Hiftorians mention the Murder of this Prince, and the miraculous manner of
its Difcovery   Concerning the latter, *William of Malmesbury*
and *Matthew of Weftminfter,* give the following legendary Account, *viz.* " That after the Perpetration of this bloody Deed,
" the inhuman Sifter foon feized the Kingdom,' and prohibited
" all Enquiry after her loft Brother   But this horrible Fact,
" concealed in *England,* was made known at *Rome,* by a fu-
" pernatural Revelation, for on the Altar of St. *Peter* there,
" a White Dove let fall a Paper, on which, in golden Letters,
" was infcribed both the Death of *Kenelm,* and the Place of
" his Burial *viz.*—In (3) *Clent Cow-batch, Kenelme* King bearne,
" lieth under a Thorne, heaved, bereaved "

---

(1) Trinepos Wibbæ patris Pendæ   *Mat
of Weftm nfter,* p 221
(2) Kenelmus occifus ab Afkeberto ejus
nutritio et procuratore confilio Quendridæ in
valle de Clent   *Leland Coll: ?* v 1 p 212.

(3) Clent ex vacca alba, indice fepulchri
Kenelmi, Cowdale vulgo appellata
" *In Clent fub fpina jacet in convalle bovina,*
" *Vertice truncatus Kinelmus rege creatus*

H   *Tyrrel*

Tyrrel thus renders into our *English* this *Saxon* Inscription

" In (*) Clent *Cow-pasture, under a Thorn,*
" *Of Head bereft,* lies Kenelm, *King born* "

' The *Roman* Priests and Monks could not understand the
" Characters, but an *Englishman*, being accidentally present,
" read the Inscription, and translated it into *Latin*, whereupon
" the *Pope* sent over an Envoy to the *English* Kings, to in-
" form them concerning the murdered *Kenelm*. The Affair
' being thus miraculously revealed, the Body was taken out
" of the Hole where it had been hid, and with great Solemnity
" carried to *Winchelcombe* in *Glocestershire*, and there interred
" in the Church of that Abbey, which his Father had founded,
" Soon afterwards Pilgrimages were made to his Tomb, and
" *Camden* says, that it is scarcely credible in what great Re-
" pute *Winchelcombe* Monastery was in, on account of this Royal
" Saint '

The unnatural Sister did not long enjoy the Fruit of her
ambitious Cruelty, for she was ousted from the Throne by her
Uncle *Ceolwulf*, in a few Months after her Brother was killed.

St MILBURGA, Daughter of *Meravaldus*, the fourth Son
of King *Penda*, a near Kinswoman to St *Herburgh*,

(*) Clent is famed on account such
Places of Martyrdom adjoining to it.
Near to this Place is a famous | Spring called St *Kenelm's Well* to which
extraordinary Virtues have been attributed

BEORNA. This Name, as upon the Scroll, or Label, is *FIG 11* not in the Catalogue of the Sovereigns of *Mercia*, tho' we meet with it among the Kings of the *East-Angles*, over whom one *Beorna* reigned, and lived in the Time of St. *Werburgh*.

COLWLPHUS (commonly wrote CEOLWULF) was Bro- *FIG 12* ther of King *Kenulf*, and Uncle to the assassinated *Kenelm*. He drove his barbarous Niece *Quendrida*, from the *Mercian* Throne, and began to reign A. D. 840, but in his second Year, *Sax Chron* he himself was defeated, and forced out of his Territories, by an Usurper, named *Beornwulph*. He left only one Daughter, cal- *Spelmans Councils, p 333* led *Kenedritha*.

Sta ⸺⸺LDA. From the three only remaining Letters *FIG 14* of the Name upon this Label, we may reasonably conjecture, that this female Saint was intended to represent *Erminilda*, Mother of St. *Werburgh*, and Daughter of *Ercombert*, King *Sax Chron sub ann 640* of *Kent*, by his Wife *Sexburga*, Princess of the *East-Angles*. *Ercombert* was a zealous Christian, destroyed Heathen Idols and demolished their Temples. He instituted the Observance of *Lent* in his Kingdom, and was (faith *Malmesbury*) " famous " for his Piety towards God, and his Love to his Country." He married his Daughter (*) *Erminilda* to *Wulphere*, King of *Mercia*, by whom she had *Werburgha* and other Children.

(*) Erminilda, filia S Sexburghæ, nupsit | Werburgham —*Ex libello de genealogia et vi* Wulphero, regi Merciorum, ex quo genui | *ta S Etheldreiæ*

After

After her Husband's Death, she, and her Daughter *Wir-burgha*, were veiled by her Aunt *Etheldreda*, Abbess of *Ely*, (1) and thence she went to *Shepie* (in *Kent*) of which, she was, by her Mother *Sexburga*, appointed Abbess. She afterwards succeeded her Aunt in the Abbey of *Ely*, (2) where she died, and was buried.—She is said to have founded the Priory of *Stone* in *Staffordshire*, but others attribute it to her Husband, King *Wulphere*.

Fig. 15 REX - - - - - - - - DUS. This Statue has the Stile of King, yet holds a Crosier in one Hand, by which Tokens, corroborated by the remaining Syllable on the Label, it may be supposed to have been the Effigies of *Ethelraus*, Uncle to St *Werburgh*, and Successor to his Brother *Wulphere*, in the Kingdom of *Mercia*. Though he seems to have taken upon him the Government, as his Nephew *Kenred* was so very young at his Father's Death, yet he held the reins rather too long for a Regency.

Soon after his taking the Crown (3) he ravaged the Kingdom of *Kent*, and destroyed most of the Churches, Monasteries, and Possessions belonging to the See of *Rochester*. He then entered into a War with *Egfrid*, King of the *Northumbers*, and conquered the much greater Part of *Lincolnshire*, which was confirmed to him by Treaty. The venerable Historian

---

Mortuo Wulphero Ermenilda venit ad Scepege et a Sexburga, matre Abba fatia et Ex eam

Cum Ermenilda et sepula est in El Ex eam

(2) Sancta Ermenilda apud Hely pauiat *Malmesb*,

(3) Etheldredus rex Merc. Cantiam vaf a nt unde Rouce ria destru ta *Lil d Collect*. v 1 p 17

tells us, that he afterwards began to be religiously disposed, and to compensate for his Devastations in the Diocese of *Rochester*, he erected a Bishoprick at *Worcester*, and was a great Benefactor to the Abbey of *Peterborough*, and delivering up the Kingdom to the rightful Heir *Kenred*, he became Abbot of the Monastery of *Bardeney* in *Lincolnshire*, where he died, and was buried.

Sir Peter Leycester, p 93.
Sax Chron sub ann 675
Bede, l v, ch 19
Sax Chron. A D 716

Sta - - - - - - RGA. By the Termination upon the Scroll, and the Number of Letters required to fill up the Space, this Figure may be conjectured to have represented St. *Keneburga*, who was Sister to King *Wulphere*, and Aunt to St. *Werburgh*. She was married to *Adelwal*, Prince of the *Northumbers*, and was a considerable Benefactress to the Monastery of *Peterborough* After the Death of her Husband she took the Veil, and was much esteemed for her eminent Piety. About three hundred Years after her Death, her Bones were dug up by *Ælfius*, Abbot of *Peterborough*, and buried in that Monastery.

FIG 17

Sax Chron sub ann 675

Sax Chron sub anno 963

- - - - - US. This Image holds in its Right Hand a Pastoral Staff, and may, from the Character and Disposition of that Prince, not improbably, be supposed to represent *Konredus*, Brother to St. *Werburgh*, who is, more than once, mentioned under *Fig* 16 His being a helpless Infant at his Father's Death, induced his Uncle *Ethelred* to assume the Government, as has been before taken Notice of. His Uncle's continuing on the Throne did not seem to affect him, who was allowed

FIG 18.

to

to be much fitter for a Cloyster than for a Co..t   After he had reigned about five Years, he relinquished the Crown to his Cousin-German *C..r..*, before-mentioned, went to *Rome*, accepted of an Abbacy, h.. passed the Rem..... of his Days .... in the Monastery of S.. *....*, in t... C.ty

BALDREDUS. N.. .. T.. ....g the *Mercian* P...... .... N..., w.o was the last of t.e King.. of K.. .. F. *King*, King of *M...*, having conquered .... Kingcom (A D 7..) app..ted *..t.l..d*, a *M..... N.b...a.*, to govern there, and upon His Dece.. te, per...d... S.. *B....*, to succeed him, who having reigned n... eighteen Ye.rs, w.s attacked ... .ted by *Egbert*, reputed the first Monarch of *En.l..d*, who drove ... out of his Territor.es, ... was never heard .. after..... (*)

MERWALDUS called MERWALA in the S..on *Annals*, when Chron.... ....es with *M.m..bury Si..on of D.l...m*, ... *B.... of h..... .... de .. H.Son of King *T...* ... Father of S. *M.....* S. *M....ls*, and St *M.....* and ... *..c.. S. ....*, His .l.er Brother *E..l.d* as .... as he c... .. .. Th.. of *M....*, erected *H....d* ... . it to *M.r......* .... D.... .... *K.ng of K..t*, b. whe. he h.. the three Daughters before-mentioned, but no M.. I...

WIGLAFF, commonly called WITLAFF, and by the *Saxon Chronicle*, WITHLAFF, was a great Chieftain, or Eolderman, among the *Mercians*, and by them (after the Royal Line was extinct) advanced to the sovereign Power. *Florence of Worcester* stiles him (*) a Petty King in the western Part of *Mercia*. Two Years after his Promotion, the great *Saxon* Prince, *Egbert*, having reduced most of *Mercia*, marched an Army against *Wiglaff*, and drove him out of his Territory. The vanquished Prince fled to the Abbey of *Croyland*, and was concealed for three or four Months, in his Cousin *Etheldreda*'s Cell, at length, by the Mediation of *Siward*, Abbot of that Monastery, he was restored to his Sovereignty, and permitted to enjoy it, subject to a Tribute. This King *Wiglaff* seems to have been related to St *Werburgha*, as the Historians call him the Kinsman of *Etheldreda*, who was Aunt to *Erminilda*, the Mother of *Werburgha*.

FIG 22
Leland Coll
Malmesbury,
l 1 ch 4

Sax Chron
sub ann. 825.

Brompton, p.
776

Ingulphus

BERTWULPH. He was the Brother of *Wiglaff*, and began to reign A D 839, but was admitted to his Government, only as a tributary Prince under *Igbert* the *Saxon* His Rule continued for about twelve or thirteen Years, when the *Danes*, in three hundred Ships, came up the *Thames*, and making a Descent, took *Canterbury* and *London*, and defeating *Bertwulph*'s Army, drove him out of *Mercia*, and forced him to take Refuge abroad

FIG 23
Leland Coll.

Sax Chron
sub ann 851.

(*) In occiden ali plaga Merciorum regulu

Rex

BURGHREDUS He was permitted to succeed Bert-
....', upon the like tributary Tenure, A D 852. He is
mentioned (by the Stile of *Rex*) to have been present, along
with many other Princes, at the Endowment of (1) *Medeßam-
..a* Monaftery He (2) married *E.h.l..ida*, Daughter of *Etlel-
wulph*, or *Aaalun'f*, the *Saxon* Monarch, who, upon an Ap-
plication from his Son-n-law, and the *Mercian* Nobility, entered into an Alliance with him, to affift him in his Wars againft
the *Wel.*, and he accordingly marched a powerful Army
through *Mercia*, and warred againft the *Welß* with fo much
Succefs, that he obliged them to come to *Burghred's* own Terms.

After he had continued in the Government of *Mercia* twenty-
two Years, he was over-powered, and defeated by the *Danes*,
and being forced to fly beyond the Seas, he took Refuge at
Rome, where he ended his Days in the *Englifb* Seminary, and
was buried in their Church, dedicated to the Bleffed Virgin.

S.-------EDA By the Remains on the defaced Label
belonging to this Image it may be conjectured, that it was intended for St *Lilludreaa* who was Great-Aurt to St *Werburgh a*, and velled her and her Mother *Erminilda*, at her Abbey
of *E.* This *Etb.lda* as was Daughter of *Anna*, King of the
Eaft-angle., (..) and Widow of *Torbit*, a Prince in the fouth-

---

.... .us ron-ono cum duodecim an
.... .ut reg.... Sub ium .... pe... ar.er mund.t virgini
Burgreds.n Memor.m .... .t.. .... regn.a glor.o'a B.de l. n ch i.
... ...nter ....n.. .... n Reg. i

ern (1) Parts of *Northumberland*, and afterwards married to *Egfrid*, King of the *Northumbers*, with whom she lived twelve Years, yet still preserv'd her Virginity. She took the Veil from St. *Ebba*, Abbess of *Coldingham*, and soon after became (2) Abbess of *Ely*, where she died, and was buried A. D. 679.

A D 671
Bede
Sax Chron
fub annis
673 & 679

ETHELBERTUS. There was no *Mercian* King of this Name, but several in other Kingdoms during the Heptarchy. Among these was *Ethelbert*, King of *Kent*, who was one of the most celebrated Princes of his Time, and the first Christian King of his Nation. Having founded several Sees, he died in the fifty-sixth Year of his Reign

FIG 29

Sax Chron
fub annis 60,
604, 616

Ethelbert was Great Great-Grandfather to S. *Werburgh*, his Grandson *Ercombert*'s Daughter, *Erminilda*, being her Mother.

Sᵗᵃ MILDRIDA. This Princess is taken Notice of, under *Fig* 21, as Daughter of *Merwaldus*, and Cousin-German to St *Werburgh*. Little or nothing else concerning her, is mentioned by any of our Historians.

FIG

We have now gone thorough with the proposed Historical Sketches relating to each of their Images, whose represented Original could be ascertained by its Label, and have supplied some of the defaced Ones with such Conjectures, as (it is hoped) will not be deemed irrational or improbable.

---

(1) Longo ut Australium Girvior m erat *Ireland Collect* s i p 212
princess, p nus S Ltad'nie tari | z) Ipsa facta est Abbatissa in regione qua
Egr dus autem rex Northumbr ke n a | vocatur Lige *Bed*, u anrea

The Memoirs of the *Mercian* Saints might have been a good deal enlarged, but the *Legendary* and *Miraculous* have been studiously avoided, and of these Sort of Anecdotes, but a single Specimen is given, *viz.* in the Account of that young Saint, the murder'd *Kenelm.*

There would likewise have been a more ample Mention of our Virgin Patroness, St. *Werburh,* but that only a Summary, not a History is intended. Yet in the preceding Pages some other Excellences will appear, as well as her Royal Lineage and High Extraction. She being descended from, and allied to, not only the *Mercian* Monarchs, but also the Kings of *Kent,* those of the *East-Angles,* and other Potentates of the *Saxon* Heptarchy. And the liberal Benefactions of the renowned (1) *Etheldred* and *Ethelfleda,* the Charter of King (2) *Edgar,* the Munificence of (3) *Leofric* and his Lady *Godiva,* and the like Endowments of (4) our famous *Hugh Lupus,* his Countess *Ermentrude,* and his *Barons,* together with the Confirmations

---

1 There were Springs of ... for to make the Date of ... to be A. D. 858, ... the Beginning ... the Ninth Century, which ... one hundred Years before ... Him ... F ... began his Reign. This king was at ... She was the Daughter of ... *Cenred* A. D. ... and died ... D. 975, in ... ... in the ... Year of his Age

... Monasterii ... nupt ... Leofricus Comes reparavit Monasteri-
... *Leland Coll* ... in *Werburge* Cestriæ *Leland Collecton*
...

... The Donations of ... ... He was Earl of *Mercia* ... A. D. 1018
... ... C ... was ... remarkable Benefactress ... Virg ... in the City of Coventry mentioned by several ...
... ... History ...
... ... *Leofricus Comes* templum in honorem ...
Some Parts of the old Charter ... ... *sanctæ* Virginis posuit quod postea ...
perhaps no very agreeable ... have occa ... *Hugo primus è Normannico genere* Cestriæ
sioned Sir *Henry Dugdale's* ... ... *Comes* instauravit. *Camden Britan.* p. 467

and

and additional Bounties of the succeeding Earls of *Chester*, will sufficiently evince the great Respect and Veneration which After-Ages had for the Memory of this devout and exemplary Princess.

As the Shrine of this Saint, and its curious Decorations here treated of, have not been touched upon by any of our Writers, perhaps, even these hasty Collections may be of Service to some future Compiler, who may possibly undertake to give us the History and Antiquities of the Churches and City of *Chester*.

FINIS.